THE LOST TREASURE OF LARRY LONGFOOT

BY CARI MEISTER • ILLUSTRATED BY ADAM RECORD

LEARNING TO USE A MAP

PICTURE WINDOW BOOKS
a capstone imprint

egend says that the pirate Longfoot buried his treasure on Boot Island. And I, Cap'n Cal, have the treasure map!

PIRATES FOR HIRE

MASKED MARVIN
• SHARK LOVER
• SEA-SHANTY SINGER
• ACCORDION PLAYER

HEIDI HEY
• GREAT DECK-SWABBER
• MAP EXPERT
• TIGHTROPE WALKER

JIM "THE NOSE" JAM
• KNIFE-THROWING CHAMP
• TRAP SETTER
• CAN SMELL TROUBLE

But I have a problem—I don't know how to read a map. I need help. Which pirate should I bring with me on my adventure?

I PICK HEIDI.
CAN YOU
GUESS WHY?

When I track down Heidi, I ask her to come to Boot Island with me.

Her eyes grow large. "Are you crazy?" she asks. "Haven't you heard about Jaguar Jungle, Madman's Maze, Leech Lake, and Creepy Cave Tunnel?"

"Yes," I say. "Have you heard of Captain Longfoot? The pirate that had more jewels than the king himself?"

Heidi smiles and looks at her feet. "Yes, I have."

"I have his treasure map," I say.

"What are we waiting for?" yells Heidi. "Let's go!"

We board my ship, and I steer it toward Boot Island.

Heidi sees me staring at the map. "Need some help?" she asks.

She takes the map from my hand. "You had
it upside-down," she says. "Let's make a deal. I'll
teach you map skills if you share the treasure."

"Deal," I say.

We shake on it—pirate style.

"This is called the compass rose," Heidi says. "It shows the cardinal directions: north, south, east, and west. We will be coming to the island from the north. I've drawn a dashed line on the map to mark our course.

BOOT ISLAND

Leech Lake

Larry's Lagoon

Jaguar Jungle

Monkey Rock

Creepy Cave Tunnel

N

E

S

COMPASS ROSE

"On the top right is the legend. It tells us what the symbols mean."

"So, the legend is the key?" I say with a smile.

"Exactly!" says Heidi. "See that symbol that looks like a tree? When you see that symbol on the map, it means there are trees there."

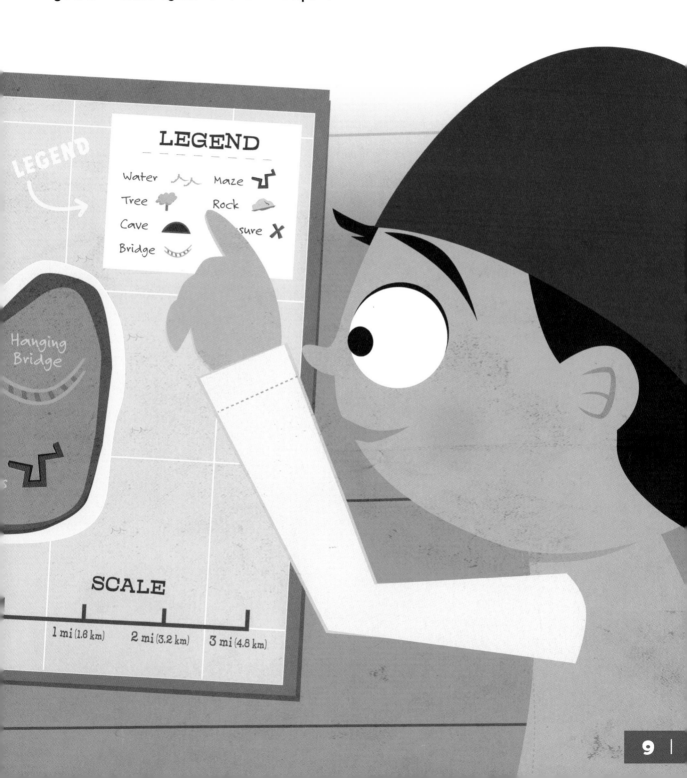

"I see Larry's Lagoon," says Heidi. "See how the shape of the land goes around the water like a bowl? And see the Jaguar Jungle?"

"They're so much bigger than they look on the map," I say.

"Every part of a map is shrunk by the same amount," explains Heidi. "Because the world is round and maps are flat, no map will be exactly correct."

- Swab the poop deck.
- Sea shanty sing-along.
- Batten down the hatches.
- Hoist the Jolly Roger.
- Walk the plank.
- Avoid Davy Jones' Locker.
- Avast scallywags!
- Yo, Ho, Ho Aaaarrrr!
- Find buried treasure!

shiver me timbers & heave ho!

weigh anchor and hoist th...

BOOT ISLAND

Leech Lake

Larry's Lagoon

Jaguar Jungle

Monkey Rock

Madma Maze

Creepy Cave Tunnel

W ·· N ·· E ·· S

"What's that big X?" I ask.

Heidi points to the legend.

"Oh!" I say. "The treasure! It's buried on the west side of the island."

"Good," says Heidi. "You're becoming a map expert."

"We can use the scale on the map to figure out how far away we are from the treasure," says Heidi. "The scale on the map compares distances on land to distances on the map."

LEGEND

Water   Maze

Tree   Rock

Cave   Treasure   X

Bridge

Place a ruler on the map, and mark the distance between two spots. One inch (2.5 centimeters) on the map equals 1 mile (1.6 kilometers) on Earth. Heidi and Cal are about 2.5 miles (4 km) away from the treasure!

SCALE

(1.6 km)   2 mi (3.2 km)   3 mi (4.8 km)

We head ashore. There are many different paths to take. We decide to take the path south toward Jaguar Jungle.

GRRR!

"YIKES!" I SAY. "IS THERE ANOTHER WAY?"

GRRR!

GRRR!

Heidi checks the map. "You want to go across Leech Lake?" she asks.

I nod. I like to swim. I get one look at the leeches and change my mind.

BLOOD-SUCKING LEECHES

We decide to head east to the hanging bridge. I take one look at the bridge and I get really scared. "I can't do it!" I say. "I'm scared of heights!"

Heidi blindfolds me and leads me across. When we step off the bridge, we are at Madman's Maze.

A compass is an instrument people use to figure out direction. It has a needle that points north.

COMPASS

"This maze looks tricky," Heidi says. "But if you look at the map, the treasure is west of the maze. We can use our compass to keep walking west."

Finally, we make it out of the maze.

Next we have to go through Creepy Cave Tunnel. I want
to turn back, but I'm brave and we make it through.
"How do we know EXACTLY where to dig?" I ask Heidi.
"There is no big X on the sand."

BOOT ISLAND

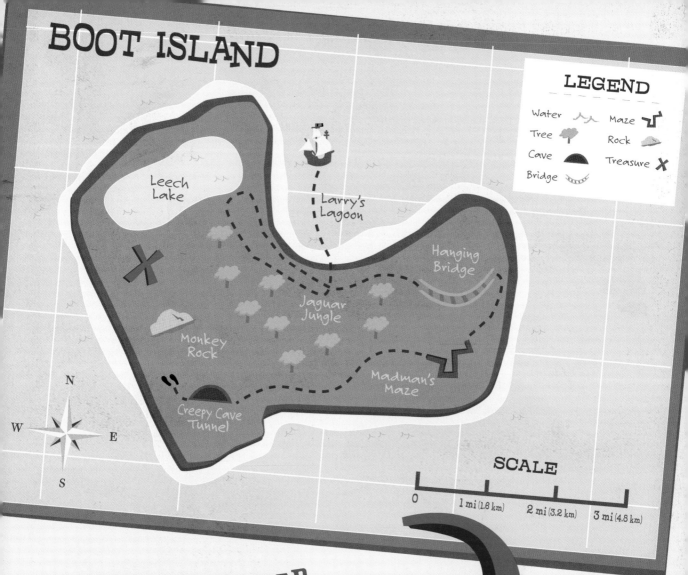

LEGEND

Water | Maze
Tree | Rock
Cave | Treasure
Bridge

Leech Lake

Larry's Lagoon

Hanging Bridge

Jaguar Jungle

Monkey Rock

Madman's Maze

Creepy Cave Tunnel

N W E S

SCALE

0   1 mi (1.6 km)   2 mi (3.2 km)   3 mi (4.8 km)

SHE FLIPS tHE MAP OVER AND READS.

After the Creepy Cave Tunnel, take 10 giant steps to the northwest. When you see a monkey-shaped rock, walk 10 more giant steps to the northwest. Then dig.

Heidi and I follow the directions. We finally find the spot where the X is on the map. And then we dig, and dig, and dig ...

Heidi's shovel hits something hard. "We found it!" she yells.

"Look at all the gold!" I say as I open the chest.

"Look at the books!" says Heidi. "My grandfather must've buried them with his treasure."

"Your Grandfather?" I ask. And that's when I see her LONG feet.

"My grandpa was Larry Longfoot," she explains. "He buried his treasure before his ship went down. I thought the map went with it."

"I should have guessed!" I say.

"You can have the gold. I just want the books." says Heidi. "Thank you Cap'n Cal!"

But Heidi knows as well as I do, that I couldn't have read that map and found the treasure without her.

BURY A TREASURE!

Find a shoebox. Decorate it and fill it with treasure. Ask an adult to help you bury it. Make a treasure map to remember where you hid your treasure. Be sure to include a compass rose, cardinal directions, a legend, and symbols.

What you need:

- a shoebox
- markers or stickers for decorating
- some kind of treasure
- a plastic shovel
- paper
- a pen or pencil

GLOSSARY

cardinal directions—the four main points toward which something can face: north, south, east, and west

compass rose—a label that shows direction on a map

legend—a part of a map that shows what the symbols on the map stand for; a legend is also called a key; a legend can also be a story passed on from earlier times

scale—a label on a map that compares the distances on a map and the actual distances on Earth

symbol—a design or picture on a map that stands for something else

READ MORE

Gonzales, Doreen. *Are We There Yet?: Using Map Scales.* Map Mania. Mankato, Minn.: Capstone Press, 2008.

Olien, Rebecca. *Map Keys.* Rookie Read-About Geography. New York: Children's Press, 2013.

Waldron, Melanie. *How to Read a Map.* Let's Get Mapping! Chicago: Capstone Raintree, 2013.

INDEX

INTERNET SITES

FactHound offers a safe, fun way to find Internet sites related to this book. All of the sites on FactHound have been researched by our staff.

Here's all you do:

Visit *www.facthound.com*

Type in this code: 9781404883055

Super-cool stuff! Check out projects, games and lots more at **www.capstonekids.com**

Thanks to our advisers for their expertise, research, and advice:

Professor Robert E. Roth, PhD, Professor of Geography
University of Wisconsin, Madison

Terry Flaherty, PhD, Professor of English
Minnesota State University, Mankato

Editor: Shelly Lyons
Designer: Alison Thiele
Art Director: Nathan Gassman
Production Specialist: Jennifer Walker
The illustrations in this book were created digitally.

Picture Window Books are published by Capstone,
1710 Roe Crest Drive, North Mankato, Minnesota 56003
www.capstonepub.com

Library of Congress Cataloging-in-Publication Data
Meister, Cari.
The lost treasure of Larry Longfoot : learning to use a map/
by Cari Meister ; illustrated by Adam Record.
pages cm.—(Take it outside)
Includes index.
ISBN 978-1-4048-8305-5 (library binding)
ISBN 978-1-4795-1935-4 (paperback)
ISBN 978-1-4795-1896-8 (ebook pdf)
1. Maps—Juvenile literature. I. Record, Adam illustrator.
II. Title.
GA105.6.M47 2014
 912—dc23   2013006273

Printed in the United States of America in
Stevens Point, Wisconsin.
032013   007227WZF13

LOOK FOR ALL THE BOOKS IN THE TAKE IT OUTSIDE SERIES: